NFL NO-BRAINERS:

REALIGNMENT & NCAA UNIVERSITY

I0159302

BOOKS BY BRYANT T. JORDAN

Saving the Lakers: A Be the General Manager Book

Saving the Celtics: A Be the General Manager Book

An Open Letter to ALL Regarding Donald Sterling

NFL No-Brainers: Realignment & NCAA University

NFL NO-BRAINERS:

REALIGNMENT & NCAA UNIVERSITY

————————◊————————

Bryant T. Jordan

Sports Seer Publishing LLC

NFL No-Brainers: Realignment & NCAA University

© 2014 by Bryant T. Jordan

All rights reserved. No portion of this book may be reproduced in any form without prior written permission of the publisher or author. Scripture quotations are taken from the King James Version of the Bible.

Published by Sports Seer Publishing LLC

Library and Archives Canada Cataloguing in Publication

Jordan, Bryant T., 1979-, author
    NFL no-brainers : realignment & NCAA university / Bryant T. Jordan.

Issued in print and electronic formats.
ISBN 978-1-927654-37-8 (pbk.).--ISBN 978-1-927654-36-1 (pdf)

    1. National Football League. 2. National Football League--Management. 3. National Football League--Reorganization.
I. Title.

GV955.5.N35 J64 2014   796.332'64   C2014-908327-0
                                                   C2014-908328-9

For more information about this publisher, visit:
www.SportsSeerPublishing.com

For more information about this author, visit:
www.bryantTjordan.com

DEDICATED TO GOD:

FATHER, WORD AND HOLY SPIRIT

By the way, for those of you who think it strange an author of sports-centric titles would dedicate his books to God, allow me to say, God is my life and everything I do revolves around Him. I am not a writer that happens to be a Biblical Christian; I am a follower of the Lord Jesus Christ of Nazareth who happens to write and do a myriad of other things, period.

SPORTS SEER PUBLISHING LLC

Sports Seer Publishing LLC is dedicated to publishing thought-provoking and game-changing sports books for readers of all ages.

Our **www.SportsSeerPublishing.com** website is a great place for you to learn more about us and how to purchase our products.

We are also currently accepting unsolicited manuscripts. If you have written a book you believe in and believe is a saleable title containing original, thought-provoking information, we urge you to submit it to us at your earliest convenience. We would love to be able to read it and consider signing you to a new author contract if we feel the book fits our publishing goals.

ACKNOWLEDGEMENTS

As this is a small book and not much research was needed, I will keep my acknowledgements to a minimum.

I want to thank my children for their love, encouragement and patience. Each of you mean more than life itself to me!

I want to further thank my eldest son for his contributions to this book. It was our discussions and debates on NFL realignment that helped me realize this was an issue that even casual fans may have more than a passing interest in. Thank you my boy for being not only a great son but a great friend whose opinion I value.

I want to thank my amazing wife for her undying love and never ending support and help. Thank you baby; you truly are the greatest woman on earth in my mind!

Finally, my greatest debt and greatest thanks goes to the One true God of the Bible: Father, Word and Holy Spirit. Without You I am nothing and I love You with all my heart and soul.

CONTENTS

INTRODUCTION

The *National Football League* (NFL) has never been more popular; however its also never been more ridiculed. Money is flowing like water while at the same time traumatic injuries seem to be increasing at an alarming rate. Simply put, the NFL is at a crossroads.

Less than 50 years ago – in 1970 – the minimum salary for veteran players was $10,000. Today, a player that's been in the league for just one season earns a minimum salary of no less than $495,000. And, before you say that money was worth a lot more in 1970 than it is today, understand that a $10,000 salary in 1970 is the equivalent of $60,975.61 salary in 2014 and $61k is a far, far cry from $495k. Like I said, the money is flowing in the NFL!

However, in a year that saw three high school football players (Demario Harris Jr., Isaiah Langston and Tom Cutinella) die after suffering football related injuries, and 16 high school players die due to the same over the past two years, the game of football seems closer than ever to 1905, and that's not a good thing.

In 1905, a total of 19 players died from football related injuries and it's said that United States President Theodore Roosevelt threatened to ban the game entirely if player safety could not be drastically improved. In fact, Patrick B. Donohue, founder of the *The Sarah Jane Brain Foundation* wrote an article on *FoxNews.com* titled *Should President Obama Ban Football?* While Donahue would not go so far as to say football should be banned by the President, a poll on *Debate.org* noted that 59% of voters believed football should indeed be banned.

Personally I would never want any of my children to play any position other than kicker or punter if they were to play football, and even then I would be nervous watching them play. However, I am not naive enough to think I am in the majority.

Football is basically a religion in the good ole USA and the *National Football League* is its dominant denomination while Roger Goodell is its Pope. Football isn't going anywhere; in fact, it's only going to increase in popularity and salaries and earnings are only going to increase in my opinion. The USA is the modern equivalent of ancient Rome, the gridiron is the modern equivalent of the Coliseum and the players are the modern equivalent of the infamous gladiators; and it seems everyone loves a gladiator these days, be it Russell Crow in a Ridley Scott film, Jon Bones Jones in a UFC fight or Tony Romo playing an NFL game with broken ribs, a busted back and a punctured lung!

Regardless, if the NFL really wants to maximize its earnings and mass popularity – outside of doing whatever it takes to make the game safer for all who play it – there are two things I personally believe the NFL should do ASAP.

The first is to geographically realign the eight current divisions. It makes absolutely no sense that the three Florida teams (Dolphins, Buccaneers and Jaguars) are in three entirely different divisions or that the two Texas teams don't even compete in the same conference. Of course it also makes no sense that there are more Florida teams than Texas teams in the first place, but that's a different issue entirely, one that is beyond the scope of this book.

When you look at the makeup of the current NFC South, you just have to shake your head and say, *why*? There isn't a single matchup in that division that is anything close to a real and respected rivalry. Any team from Atlanta should obviously be in a division with the three Florida teams. I mean, seriously, it's as if someone at NFL Headquarters called up the Kardashian clan and asked them to pick the four teams that should be in the NFC South; the pairings are that ridiculous.

Simply put, realignment is an absolute *no-brainer* for the NFL, period.

The second thing I believe the NFL should do ASAP is form its own NCAA University. Yes, you read that right; I believe the *National Football League* should create the *NFL University.* In fact, I consider creating such a university to also be *a no-brainer* decision for Pope Goodell and the gang at 345 Park Avenue, New York, NY.

Now, in the words of the great, or at least gregarious, Terell Owens, *getcha popcorn ready* and read-on young padawan, read on!

THE CURRENT AFC EAST

NY Jets

Buffalo Bills

New England Patriots

Miami Dolphins

The current AFC East makes a great deal of sense – for three of the teams. However, having the Miami Dolphins in the same division with the Bills and Jets, let alone the Patriots, who play in a city nearly 1,500 miles from Miami, Florida, is just preposterous.

The Miami Dolphins obviously belong in a division with the other two Florida teams in the NFL – the Tampa Bay Buccaneers and Jacksonville Jaguars. That this division needs realignment is obvious.

.

THE CURRENT AFC NORTH

Cleveland Browns

Cincinnati Bengals

Pittsburgh Steelers

Baltimore Ravens

The current AFC North features in-state rivals in the Cleveland Browns and Cincinnati Bengals which is great. However having the Pittsburgh Steelers and Baltimore Ravens in the same division makes no sense.

The Pittsburgh Steelers obviously belong in the same division as the Philadelphia Eagles and the Baltimore Ravens obviously belong in the same division as the Washington Redskins. It's clear the current AFC North is in need of some serious realignment.

THE CURRENT AFC SOUTH

Indianapolis Colts

Jacksonville Jaguars

Houston Texans

Tennessee Titans

Calling the current AFC South a *mess* would be putting it lightly; calling it an absolute travesty would be more apropos. Indianapolis is over 1,000 miles from Houston, and even Nashville, Tennessee where the Titans play is nearly 600 miles from Jacksonville, Florida. The current alignment of this division makes no sense at all and needs a massive overhaul.

THE CURRENT AFC WEST

Denver Broncos

Kansas City Chiefs

Oakland Raiders

San Diego Chargers

I suppose one could say that since the current AFC West contains two teams from the same state it's better aligned than most divisions; however that wouldn't be saying much. The real truth is that this division is a geographic mess like most.

Having the Kansas City Chiefs in the same division as the Oakland Raiders – who happen to be nearly 1,800 miles away from Kansas City – is ridiculous. Having the Chiefs instead of the San Francisco 49'ers – who play in a stadium just 33 miles down the road from the Raiders stadium – in that same division is just flat out asinine!

No matter, realignment could easily turn this division into one of the most watched and talked about divisions in pro football, a division Pope Goodell could be proud of.

THE CURRENT NFC EAST

Philadelphia Eagles

NY Giants

Washington Redskins

Dallas Cowboys

Honestly it's rather difficult to think about breaking up the four teams in this division as they represent historic rivalries and have some of the most rabid fan bases in professional sports. However, there are four simple reasons to realign the storied NFC East.

First, the New York Giants simply must be in the same division as their in-state rivals the New York Jets and Buffalo Bills. Second, the Dallas Cowboys must be in the same division as their in-state rivals the Houston Texans. Third, the Philadelphia Eagles must be in the same division as their in-state rivals the Pittsburgh Steelers. Fourth, the Washington Redskins must be in the same division as the Baltimore Ravens.

All of the above said, the current NFC East is actually quite a mess geographically speaking. Realignment can fix that and create new and possibly even more heated rivalries which would be great for the league's mass popularity.

THE CURRENT NFC NORTH

Detroit Lions

Chicago Bears

Green Bay Packers

Minnesota Vikings

The NFC North is the paramount division in football today, not merely because the rivalries are incredibly intense but because the rivalries are every bit as much about geography as they are about history. You just can't create a better division than the NFC North for my money. In fact, the NFC North should be the model for all post-realignment divisions, period.

THE CURRENT NFC SOUTH

New Orleans Saints

Tampa Bay Buccaneers

Carolina Panthers

Atlanta Falcons

The current NFC South is an abomination. Not only are the four teams rather pathetic on the field – though I admit on-field success is cyclical and should not be a factor in deciding whether or not realignment is called for – the teams are not even natural rivals. The manufactured rivalries in this division are dull and simply don't excite casual fans in my opinion, and one would think that exciting casual fans should be one of the NFL's primary goals going forward.

Even casual fans seem to know the Packers hate the Bears and the Eagles hate the Redskins and that's a good thing for the NFL. The current NFC South is just devoid of any real fervor; however realignment could fix such a problem, and fast!

THE CURRENT NFC WEST

Seattle Seahawks

San Francisco 49'ers

Arizona Cardinals

Saint Louis Rams

The current NFC West is one of the most competitive divisions in football today; however it's also in serious need of realignment. Lucky for fans of the division the two best teams in the division – the San Francisco 49'ers and Seattle Seahawks – just happen to be the two teams that should stay in the division!

THE NEW AFC EAST

NY Giants

NY Jets

Buffalo Bills

New England Patriots

The new and improved AFC East is the quintessential *no-brainer* post-realignment division. Three of the four teams are current AFC East teams already and adding the New York Giants while subtracting the Miami Dolphins who obviously belong in a division with the other two Florida teams makes all the sense in the world.

I have little doubt that having all three New York teams in one division would spark an enormous amount of interest, even from casual fans which would be great for the NFL. If ever there was a *no-brainer* division, it's the new and improved AFC East.

THE NEW AFC NORTH

Cleveland Browns

Cincinnati Bengals

Indianapolis Colts

Carolina Panthers

The new AFC North would continue to feature the Cleveland Browns and Cincinnati Bengals. The Indianapolis Colts are also an obvious fit in a division with the two Ohio teams.

The Carolina Panthers may not seem like a natural fit but considering it's a mere 1,553 combined miles from Charlotte, North Carolina to both Cleveland and Cincinnati, Ohio as well as Indianapolis, Indiana – compared to the current 1,562 miles Charlotte rests from the other home cities of the three teams (Saints, Falcons and Buccaneers) in their present division known as the NFC South – they are a solid fit indeed.

The new AFC North would also feature three of the most exciting young quarterbacks in the game today in Andrew Luck, Cam Newton and Johnny Manziel – and Andy Dalton.

THE NEW AFC SOUTH

Tennessee Titans

New Orleans Saints

Dallas Cowboys

Houston Texans

The new AFC South features both Texas teams which is an obvious no-brainer. It also features the Tennessee Titans who already play in the current AFC South and the New Orleans Saints which play in a stadium a mere five hour drive from Houston, Texas. Currently the Saints play in the same division as the Carolina Panthers and for those who don't know, Charlotte, NC is a 10 hour drive from N'Awlins! *Does that make any sense at all? No!*

Obviously the old AFC South can be improved upon and the new AFC South seen above would do just that in my opinion.

THE NEW AFC WEST

Atlanta Falcons

Miami Dolphins

Tampa Bay Buccaneers

Jacksonville Jaguars

The new AFC West is similar to the new AFC East in that it is the epitome of a *no-brainer* for the NFL. That the three Florida teams are currently in three different divisions is magnificently insane.

The new AFC West would feature the three Florida teams as well as the Atlanta Falcons who play in a stadium closer to Jacksonville, Florida than any other team in the NFL, including the Carolina Panthers. Simply put, the new AFC West represents realignment nirvana.

THE NEW NFC EAST

Pittsburgh Steelers

Philadelphia Eagles

Baltimore Ravens

Washington Redskins

That the Redskins and Ravens are not in the same division at present makes no sense at all. That the two Philadelphia teams are not even in the same conference at present is just idiotic.

The new NFC East could quickly create some of the most heated rivalries in all of professional sports and have even casual fans scheduling their weekends around division battles just to make sure they catch all the action. I have no doubt Pope Goodell and the gang would love that!

THE NEW NFC NORTH

Detroit Lions

Chicago Bears

Green Bay Packers

Minnesota Vikings

The new NFC North is as you can see, the old NFC North. It's the one and only division that shouldn't change one iota.

I personally believe the rivalries in this division to be the greatest in the NFL, though my view could be colored a bit by the fact I rooted for the Detroit Lions – and my favorite player of all-time, Barry Sanders, as a youngster – and rather despised the Green Bay Packers, though I have to admit I loved Brett Favre and Reggie White and have to agree with Stephen A. Smith that Aaron Rodgers is a *bad, bad man*! Regardless, I believe the great rivalries in this division are due to the close proximity of the teams involved. Simply put, I believe all NFL divisions should be constructed on the same principle of geographic proximity as the current – and new – NFC North division is.

THE NEW NFC SOUTH

Arizona Cardinals

Denver Broncos

Saint Louis Rams

Kansas City Chiefs

The Kansas City Chiefs and Saint Louis Rams are natural rivals and should obviously be in the same division as fans from each team can drive from one city to the other in well under four hours. That these two teams are not even in the same conference, let alone division, is just absurd. As for Arizona and Denver, they are the two teams that make the most geographic sense to include in the new and improved AFC South.

The new NFC South is one of only two of the post-realignment new divisions – along with the AFC West – that feature four entirely new teams. However I have no doubt these four teams would make for a dynamic new NFC South filled with intense rivalries in no time.

THE NEW NFC WEST

Seattle Seahawks

San Francisco 49'ers

Oakland Raiders

San Diego Chargers

The new NFC West is yet another *no-brainer* for the NFL. That the three California teams are not in the same division – in fact they're not even in the same conference – is obscene, just obscene. Seattle of course is a bit of an outlier when compared to every other team in the entire NFL as its stadium is no closer than a 13 plus hour drive from any other. However, Seattle is closest to San Francisco and therefore belongs in no other division than the new NFC West aka the *California division*.

The new NFC West would be yet another quintessential *no-brainer* division. The rivalries would be incredible!

THE NEED FOR AN NFL UNIVERSITY

The *National Collegiate Athletic Association* better known as the NCAA is a joke, an absolute joke. From suspending players like Todd Gurley for simply earning money from signing their own names while allowing non-sports playing students to earn money in just about any way possible, to refusing to suspend coaches for far more egregious offences than suspended players have committed, the NCAA is the *Big Brother*, mentally handicapped blind *Big Brother* that is. However, despite the many failings and damning actions of the NCAA, it's a massive cash cow, period.

As licensed attorney and freelance writer Alicia Jessop wrote in her article for *Forbes* titled, *The Economics of College Football: A Look at the Top-25 Teams' Revenues and Expenses*:

Much has been said during the college football off-season about the business of college football. Athletics departments continue to build new and expensive practice facilities and stadiums. Conferences continue to swap partners and launch lucrative bowl games. And of course, all of this occurs amidst growing discussions over whether student-athletes should be compensated and the nobility of the NCAA's plight of amateurism. In the midst of all of this, though, one thing is certain: When it comes to money, teams ranked in USA Today's pre-season top-25 poll do a great job spending it and generating it.

In fact, according to the Department of Education, the University of Alabama generated a net profit of over $45,000,000 in *football revenue* alone during the 2012 season. This said, a program like the Crimson Tide could make a net profit of over $180,000,000 over a four year span, yet pay its star quarterback exactly *nothing, zero, nada,* over the same time period. In the words of *ESPN* analysts Tom Jackson and Chris *Boomer* Berman, *Come on Man*!

The NCAA may be anything but fair and just, but I doubt anyone with any understanding of the NFL's inner workings honestly believes the NFL is overly concerned with fairness or justice either. The NFL is a billion dollar business concerned with its bottom line, period. As such, I believe the NFL would be remiss if they don't at least consider forming their own NCAA University, the *NFL University*.

Furthermore, I will also say that I personally believe an *NFL University* would benefit the so-called student athletes much more than attending a traditional institution of higher learning would. Allow me to explain:

When I envision an *NFL University* I envision a university where every student is a prospective professional football player, agent or executive. A University where each and every *student athlete* is required to take and pass courses that will further his or her goal of becoming a professional football player, agent or executive, only.

Just as medical or law school students are not required to learn how to play football or lift weights like a professional athlete, so to would no NFL University student be required to learn history, political science, earth science, calculus and the like. NFL University students will simply be required to take and pass classes that have to do with their major, which of course is the field of *professional sports.*

I envision classes that will teach students how to excel in football, how to develop their bodies to the best of their ability, how to manage the financial windfall that is coming their way, how to communicate and therefore prepare for a life after football as a sports commentator or analyst, and how to excel as a coach, scout or executive in professional sports. There is simply no legitimate reason why a student whose only goal is to work in professional sports in some capacity, need learn quantum physics or even American history as far as I'm concerned. I believe student athletes have been discriminated against for years when compared with normal non-athlete students, and that an NFL University could be the perfect place for such student athletes to grow as individuals and truly educate themselves in a way that will actually benefit them personally and improve their career earnings potential. And that, in my mind, should be the primary goal of every institution of higher learning.

Of course, I believe just about every university with a big-time college football program would be opposed to an NFL University as they would know that the vast majority of five star recruits would enroll in such a university. However, it really wouldn't be all that much different than the University of Kentucky in Men's Collegiate Basketball (though for the record I also believe the *National Basketball Association* should form an *NBA University* in the future as well). Regardless, the NCAA isn't necessarily opposed to one University dominating the competition year in and year out (see UCLA Men's Basketball from 1963-1975) and would surely recognize the enormous value an NFL University would bring to the NCAA.

In fact, with the new *College Football Playoff* system in place and therefore a greater emphasis placed on difficulty of schedule than on a team's mere won loss record, the NFL University could set itself up as an Independent team devoid of Conference affiliation and schedule 13 games against pre-season Top 25 teams to make everyone happy. I can also almost guarantee that every time the NFL University is in town for a game, the host stadium will sell out quickly, and that's never a bad thing in the NCAA's eyes.

I would also like to see this NFL University, rather than paying its players (though, for the record I do believe college players should be paid and that high school students should be offered contracts by colleges as if they were rookies entering the NFL), simply acquire massive insurance policies for each player, so that if any player on the roster suffers an injury that affects his projected draft position – let alone ends his career – such a player would be compensated accordingly.

The pros so far outweigh the cons in establishing an NFL University that I personally consider it a *no-brainer* decision for the NFL, period.

THE FUTURE OF THE NFL

By 2035 I believe the NFL will look drastically different than it does today. Not only do I believe the divisions will be geographically realigned to increase fan participation and ticket sales, I also believe the NFL will have an NCAA University where it can develop student athletes minds and bodies to better maximize their earnings potential in the arena of professional sports.

I believe the regular season schedule will increase from the current 16 games to an 18 game schedule and that there will be at least one new European and one new Canadian team in the league. I also believe each Conference will have eight playoff teams rather than the current six.

I believe the *NFL University* will be the preeminent football program in the NCAA and a perennial *College Football Playoff* participant, one that will offer the highest possible *salaries* to five-star high school graduates and overseas athletic prospects. I also believe that such a University will head up one of just two NCAA power conferences, comprised of teams that regularly obliterate their competition and surrounded by various other non-power-conferences that will be little more than the sisters of the poor and an afterthought amongst the vast majority of college football fans, let alone the *College Football Playoff* selection committee.

In regards to actual on-field play, I believe the NFL will eliminate kickoffs and extra points entirely, with teams simply starting each possession at the twenty-five yard line and also being required to attempt a one point conversion after each touchdown. I also believe that punt returns will be eliminated via a rule that spots a punted ball at the yardage marker where it first touches the field. Furthermore, I believe the current overtime rules will be changed to resemble current NCAA overtime rules, with the one exception being that each NFL team will receive one possession starting at the fifty-yard line.

I believe that the superstar running back will be a thing of the past, unless such running back is a dual-threat in the Marshall Faulk (the most under-rated running back in NFL history in my opinion) mold. I also believe that two-way players will become commonplace, with the majority being dual cornerbacks and wide-receivers. I also believe the vast majority of teams will carry only one kicker – who will also serve as its punter (thanks to the rule change regarding where punts are downed) – on their roster.

I even believe that helmets will become entirely see-through so that fans can feel as connected to their gridiron heroes as NBA fans feel to their hardwood heroes. And, I believe that the *fun* will be put back into the *No Fun League*, with player celebrations being not just allowed but promoted.

As you can see, I believe the NFL needs to change, will change, and in changing, will continue to be the most watched sport in America. Of course, such a belief could be little more than wishful thinking if superstars start dying on the field which I believe they will in the future, and if Pope Goodell and whoever succeeds him on the NFL throne continues to proclaim football and moral infallibility, and hand out unjust punishments that expose the league's utter hypocrisy. However, that's a subject for another author to tackle; I'm done.

Q & A WITH BRYANT T. JORDAN

Q: Why did you write this book?

A: After watching some sports show – most likely *Pardon the Interruption* – with my eldest boy, and hearing the show's hosts discuss realignment, my son wanted me to type out our ideas for how the eight NFL divisions should look. I did so and then figured I might as well turn such into a small book, you know, this one.

Q: Do you think anyone, let alone the NFL will take the advice and opinions you present in this book to heart?

A: Honestly I don't know and don't care. I believe a great many fans would agree with me that the NFL divisions should be based on geography and since the NFL is obviously in the business of making decisions based on their fans personal wants and desires, you never know. Regardless, I wrote this little book for fun and had a blast writing it, so that's enough for me.

Q: What do you think about the NFL's disciplinary actions against players like Adrian Peterson, Ray Rice, et al?

A: Honestly I have a serious problem with mob rule. I also do not believe that any individual should allow public opinion or political correctness to influence his or her decision making. That said I do understand the *National Football League* is a business dedicated to increasing its bottom line and that they feel the best way to do that is to roll with the masses, whether or not doing such would be hypocritical or even unjust.

Q: So, would you have suspended players like Ray Rice, Adrian Peterson, et al?

A: I don't condone abuse of any kind though I also believe the best course of action would be to allow the judicial process to play out since I strongly believe a person is *innocent until proven guilty*. However, it appears as though the majority of American citizens no longer believes in such a principle, which is a bit baffling to me and which I believe could lead to an enormous can of worms being opened in the near future. I don't know about you but I'm not looking forward to the *Thought Police* knocking on my door any time soon.

Q: Who do you believe is the *greatest* Quarterback of all-time in regards to career accomplishments?

A: Since career accomplishments which would include t-e-a-m success are being factored in, I will say Otto Graham is the *greatest* QB of all time and it's not even close. The guy won seven titles in ten seasons and never missed playing for a championship, not one single time; think about that. However, I will say that I don't agree with *team* success factoring into *individual* excellence and rankings for the most part. Watching Barry Sanders – the greatest pure runner the game has ever seen – toil for years on horrendously overmatched Detroit Lions squads taught me enough to know that individual excellence and team success are not even close to being one and the same.

Q: That said who do you feel is the *best* Quarterback of all-time?

A: Honestly, give me Aaron Rodgers. There may have been better pure passers and better scramblers but when you add everything up I'll take Rodgers over anyone, ever, period. The guy has better than a 4-to-1 career TD to INT ratio, the highest QB Rating in the history of the NFL and has already rushed for more career yards than Joe Montana and Brett Favre. Steve Young is the only guy I think of that comes close to Rodgers as far as being the total package but he only had four outstanding years over his entire career and just didn't have the longevity that I believe Rodgers will have, and actually already has had with six magnificent seasons under his belt to date. Rodgers makes the game of football look almost too easy, as if he were playing against a Madden video-game opponent rather than real live NFL defenses.

Q: So, obviously Aaron Rodgers is your favorite player of all-time, right?

A: No, not even close. I've never liked the Packers much at all and still don't. I would probably have at least 100 players and at least 15 Quarterbacks ranked ahead of Rodgers on my personal all-time favorites list. I just respect the guy and recognize his skills, period.

Q: Who do you believe is the *best* running back in NFL history?

A: I view Jim Brown as the *greatest* running back, Barry Sanders as the best *pure runner* of all-time and Marshall Faulk as the best all-around back in NFL history. I won't narrow it down any further than that.

Q: Who do you believe are the ten *best* players of all-time?

A: In order: Jim Brown, Lawrence Taylor, Reggie White, Ronnie Lott, Jerry Rice, Aaron Rodgers, Dick Butkus, Deion Sanders, Anthony Munoz and Barry Sanders with a special mention to Marshall Faulk who I believe was the best all-purpose running back in NFL history in his prime.

Q: That's sort of a strange list. So, who do you think are the ten *greatest* players of all-time?

A: In order: Otto Graham, Jim Brown, Ronnie Lott, Joe Greene, Joe Montana, Jerry Rice, Emmitt Smith, Lawrence Taylor, Peyton Manning, Tom Brady with special mentions to John Elway and Charles Hayley, the only player in league history with five Super Bowl rings.

Q: Who are your ten *favorite* players of all-time?

A: In order: Barry Sanders, Tim Tebow, Ray Lewis, Marshall Faulk, Donovan McNabb, Deion Sanders, Cam Newton, Brett Favre, Reggie White and in a tie for tenth place Drew Bledsoe and Ickey Woods.

Q: If you could change one thing about the NFL what would it be?

A: Honestly I would change the ridiculous rule that says a player can't be drafted until he's been out of high school for three years and allow NFL teams to draft kids straight out of high school. I cringe every time I see a potential superstar like Willis McGahee, Marcus Lattimore or Todd Gurley suffer a draft-status-impacting injury, let alone a career-ending one. Of course if my proposed NFL University becomes a reality that will do as such kids could receive massive insurance payouts if such an injury occurs. However, something needs to be done as the current system is extremely flawed!

Q: Who are your five greatest authors of all-time?

A: In order: God (author of the Bible), Fyodor Dostoyevsky, Leo Tolstoy, Tupac Amaru Shaur (yes I consider him an author, albeit of song lyrics and poems rather than novels and the like) and one other anonymous other who isn't on the same level as the aforementioned four, whoever that may be.

Q: Who are your five favorite authors of all-time?

A: God (author of the Bible), Tupac Amaru Shakur, Fyodor Dostoyevsky, Nancy Rue, John Grisham and Bill Simmons – sorry, I couldn't list just five.

Q: Is it true that you accurately predicted LeBron James return to the Cleveland Cavaliers months before anyone else in your *Saving the Lakers: A Be the General Manager Book*?

A: Yeah, I nailed it, absolutely nailed it. On page 154 of *Saving the Lakers: A Be the General Manager Book*, which I wrote during the 2013-14 NBA season and long before LeBron and the Heat even lost the 2014 NBA Finals to the San Antonio Spurs:

> It was shocking news when LeBron James decided to opt out of the final year of his contract with the Miami Heat and re-join the team that drafted him, especially after Cavs owner Dan Gilbert went all *Adolf* and publicly denounced James for leaving. However, the man known as *King James* was never stupid. He showed his basketball intelligence when he signed with the Heat and then went out and won multiple titles, and he showed it again this past summer when he left the aging Heat to sign with a Cavs team loaded with young talent and another legit superstar with his best days ahead of him in Kyrie Irving. And now, LeBron is once again reaping the rewards of his prudent basketball decision-making.

So, yeah, like I said, I nailed it!

Q: Cool; any last words?

A: Yeah; buy my books but more importantly serve your Creator and Saviour with all your heart and let the chips fall where they may. There's simply no better way to live your life than that.

PROLOGUE:

How a Cocky Kid from Philly Turned a Once Die-Hard Pistons Fan into a Lakers Fan and Bought Him a House to Boot

It was the summer of 1996 and I was seventeen years old. Basketball had been my first love for many years. I had skipped countless days of school to play pickup games at the local park, walked home from school upon learning that my favorite college team was playing an afternoon NCAA tournament game, and even skipped out on my second and third loves (video games and food) in order to play up to 10 hours a day that summer.

I had become quite good at the game I loved, perhaps not NBA level good but quite possibly good enough to earn a living playing professionally in an overseas league. I was a 6'2" (read 6'4" in NBA terms) combo guard who could pass the rock beautifully and rebound like a player 6" taller. I also had an incredibly diverse offensive repertoire that featured an adept post game and deadly range and accuracy on my jumper (I loved taking bets from jokers who didn't think I could hit insanely deep 3's on the playground). I still remember the first time I was over asked for an autograph - I was 12 years old and had just finished scoring every single point for my team, including many extremely deep three-pointers (for those of you who remember the University of Arkansas Razorbacks' Alex Dillard, you get the idea) during a streetball tournament game victory. I felt as if the world was mine that day and Stacey Augmon himself couldn't have stopped me (unless of course Richard Perry paid him to let me score, ahem, ahem).

Of course I was also a loose cannon that never got along with my coaches, talked a great deal of trash to opposing players, berated my own teammates for doing anything other than passing me the ball and stopped playing anything but street tournaments and blacktop games of 1-on-1 and the like long before I graduated from high school. In short, I was a prototypical knucklehead. I had visions of *walking on* at the University of Nevada Las Vegas (UNLV) and while that may not have been entirely realistic (though I do believe I could have made their 1997-98 squad as a freshman and played behind New Zealand's Mark Dickel - who could really ball by the way), I have no real doubt that I could have played Division One ball *somewhere*. Alas, playing college ball was not meant to be, and thank God for that! Instead I fell in love with the woman of my dreams, repented of my sins and gave my life to the Lord and Savior Jesus Christ of Nazareth, entered the ministry (though I now consider myself a Biblical Christian rather than any particular denomination as I am still not very fond of organized religion and would rather just serve my God, obey His word, and let the chips fall where they may), became a father of nine amazing children (at the time of this writing – who knows what the future holds) and all but gave up on actually playing the game I once loved so dearly.

There was also the matter of an irregular heartbeat, flipping out of a construction truck and landing on my back, messing up both my ankles and knees as well as my back and even later not being able to walk for quite a while due to a slipped disc in my back, but honestly all of that is beside the point. God became my first love and basketball, well, basketball is still is the *game* I love more than any other!

Enough about me and my not so illustrious hoops credentials - back to the summer of 1996. That summer was a great time to be alive, a great time to be a basketball fan and an even greater time to be a Laker fan, for that summer a new NBA dynasty was created, thanks in large part to *The Logo*, Jerry West. During the summer of 96' West pulled off perhaps the single most lop sided and some would say clairvoyant trade in the history of the NBA when he convinced the Charlotte Bobcats to trade the rights to the 13th pick in the NBA Draft (a pick the Lakers used on 17 year old Kobe Bean Bryant) for Serbian center Vlade Divac.

While many people excuse the Hornets titanic blunder, believing there was no way they could have known a mere high school kid would turn out to be the second coming of Michael Jordan and one of the three best scorers (along with Jordan and the great Wilt Chamberlain) to ever step foot on a basketball court, such isn't exactly true. The truth is that Kobe Bryant was the son of former superstar collegian and very solid NBA player Joe Bryant (who averaged 21.8 points per game and 11.4 rebounds per game on .517 shooting in his final collegiate season at LaSalle), nephew of former NBA player Chubby Cox (who was drafted by the Chicago Bulls in 1978 and last played for the Washington Bullets during the 1982-83 season - and yes that really was what his friend's called him though his birth name was John Arthur Cox III), had just finished leading a once moribund high school program (Lower Merion High School) to a state title, and even crushed the aforementioned Wilt Chamberlain's Pennsylvania high school career scoring record of 2,252 points by scoring an obscene 2,883 points. The kid known as *Bean* had even been named both the *Naismith High School Player of the Year* and the *Gatorade Men's National Basketball Player of the Year*.

Bryant was also known to have destroyed one of the NCAA's top scorers in pre-draft work-outs, a 6'8, 220 lb. small forward and grown man by the name of Dontae Jones. Jones had just finished leading the Mississippi State Bulldogs to an SEC tournament championship (which he earned MVP honors of) and an unexpected Final Four berth after being named the Regional MVP along the way. Clearly Kobe Bean Bryant was something special.

Of course, it's also true that Vlade Divac was no slouch. Divac was known as perhaps the best passing center in the league as well as one of the best passing centers of all-time. When it became common knowledge that the Hornets had never even considered drafting Bryant before trading the rights to the pick to the Lakers, it became obvious that trading for Vlade Divac was far better than drafting one of the available center prospects in the 1996 Draft such as Efthimios Rentzias or Priest Lauderdale. However, no matter how one spins it, the Bryant for Divac trade will live in infamy and may even be regarded as the beginning of *the Kobe curse* for as long as the Hornets remain a basketball team, be they in Charlotte, New Orleans, or China one day (though if they moved to China they could be called the *Dragons*, have a great mascot and serve the best sushi of any NBA team, and that alone would be cause for celebration).

Less than one month after acquiring Bryant, Jerry West would pull off the impossible and convince the most dominant physical force the game had ever seen, Shaquille O'Neal, to leave *Disney World* and the Orlando Magic for *Disney Land* and the greatest franchise in professional sports. The Los Angeles Lakers were back, *Showtime* was back and I was pumped!

Shaquille O'Neal had been my favorite player since the first time I watched him play a game at Louisiana State University. While most kids my age, and for that matter adults my size, seemed to gravitate to the guards and perhaps wing players, there was just something about the *Shaq Attack* that I found especially awesome. Although I was a natural guard who loved to shoot deep threes, I began working on my post-up game relentlessly and the first time someone called me *baby Shaq* during a pickup game I was elated.

As Shaq was my favorite player the Orlando Magic instantly became my favorite team in the summer of 92', supplanting my beloved Detroit Pistons, a team I had grown up rooting for and had season tickets to with my mother during their *Bad Boys* years. However when Shaq was drafted by the Magic, I was a Magic man through and through.

The above said, it goes without saying that when Shaq signed with the Lakers, the Lakers would instantly become my favorite team, a near sports-blasphemy for a one-time die-hard Pistons fan. However, truth be told there was something about that cocky, smiling kid from Philly that had been drafted less than a month earlier that had already had me leaning towards becoming a die-hard Lakers fan.

Over the course of the 1996-97 season something strange happened to me. Shaquille O'Neal, the great *Shaq Attack* that had been my favorite player for around seven years had become my second favorite player. The cocky, smiling kid from Philly had won my basketball heart.

Over the next six years I read just about everything I could about Kobe Bryant and quickly felt that while I had never met him we were somehow kindred spirits. I had never felt that way about Shaq, I had simply been amazed by his power and attracted to his personality but with Kobe I literally felt as if I had a personal connection, and honestly there were some interesting similarities. Kobe and I were nearly the same age, we were both thought to be extremely intelligent but also hard-headed, we each married a woman, and at an age, that our family didn't necessarily agree with, we each had a falling out with our family that wasn't caused by any overt fault of our own, we each had a me-against-the-world mentality (I used to start my days listening to *F**k the World* by *2PAC* – which honestly, even as a Christian I can still appreciate a great deal, as to be a Christian is to be in the world but not of it and therefore to have a *me-against-the-world* mentality), and of course, we were both Laker fans!

There was also a financial connection between Kobe Bryant and I, as strange as that may sound. You see, I was raised by a mother who was very wise with her money, a father who despised working for anyone but himself and a Grandmother who not only lavished me with copious financial gifts (such as giving me $250 for receiving an *A* on my report card when most of my friends might receive $5-10 for such, or $500 in bribe money to assure that I wouldn't play high school football when the only way my friends could make $500 was to work full-time for two weeks in the summer) but encouraged me to invest and increase the funds I was given rather than spend them on video games or clothes like most of my school age buddies did. All of this combined to make me, what I like to refer as, a *self-employed wise gambler*, and yes I know the term *wise gambler* sounds like an oxymoron but I was indeed a gambler and I was no moron.

I had always been interested in sports cards and sports memorabilia growing up and at one time I had some of the nicest and most valuable Shaquille O'Neal, Marshall Faulk and Drew Bledsoe collections on the planet. When Kobe Bryant came on the scene in 1996 I literally felt like I had to invest in him, just had too.

I decided to sell just about every single card and autographed jersey, ball and picture I had in my collection and use those funds, along with those I received from selling *Disney* stock and my own personal savings ($250 per A adds up pretty quick) to purchase as many Kobe Bryant *Topps Finest* rookie cards as I could get my hands on. Back then eBay wasn't very big and I had to go to local card shows almost every weekend to stock up; however after a while I had quite a stack of the gorgeous shiny bronze cards with funny peel attached called *Topps Finest*.

Had I merely held onto this stack of cards until after the Lakers 3-peat in 2002 I certainly could have turned a huge profit, however I was far too much of a gambler to just sit on such an investment. Instead I started researching ways to multiply the value of my new collection, be it through trading the cards for autographed items or even sending the cards themselves to Kobe through the mail to get autographed (generally not a good idea unless the cards you are sending are *commons* and not of significant value, or unless you enjoy losing cards, though I will say that when I wrote to Shaquille O'Neal and Tracy McGrady at one point, each player did send me an autographed item through the mail). However, what I decided to do turned out to be the best decision possible in my estimation. I had found out that the *Topps Chrome* rookie cards of Kobe, which at that time were far less valuable than the *Topps Finest* version I had a pile of, were in fact far rarer. Knowing that supply and demand is the primary factor in escalating values for items I decided straight away to trade all of my *Topps Finest* Kobe rookie cards for as many *Topps Chrome* Kobe rookie cards as I could get my hands on - and boy oh boy was I successful in doing so!

When the dust settled and I had a massive stack of the *Topps Chrome* rookie cards, which by this time were extremely coveted and selling for many times what the *Topps Finest* rookie cards were selling for, I decided that owning a home would be far more worthwhile than owning a stack of cardboard pieces with pictures on them, even if those pieces of cardboard were chrome colored and shiny and the pictures were of Kobe Bryant. Thanks to the good Lord I was able to sell that stack of sports cards and purchase my first home with my precious wife, with nothing but good ole cash money! Today I can literally and honestly say with a smile that Kobe Bryant, at least in part, bought me my first house.

INTRODUCTION

I have always been a jock but perhaps even more so a stats-geek and money-man. Ever since I was extremely young I have been a bit of a walking calculator, able to do many mathematical equations in my head faster than another can do with a calculator at his or her disposal. When I became interested in sports, it was only natural that I would instantly also become interested in player's salaries, team salary constraints and the like.

After I basically hung up my high-tops for good in order to give my ankles, knees and back a break, the financial side of the game invaded my mind even more. When websites like RealGM.com and HoopsHype.com with its team salary pages came on-line, I was in armchair GM heaven. I quickly memorized the salaries of perhaps over 100 players and began constructing trades in my head and on-paper to improve every team in the league. I also started writing on various websites and forums which almost always led to my being kicked off the site by some overzealous moderator or cyber-Nazi who happened to disagree with my opinions on his or her favorite team's problems and how to fix them with a trade that made both basketball and financial sense. Such is life.

No matter, when the urge to write a trade proposal crept up I simply searched the web for another website, and of course, used a separate pseudonym. I even ran my own sports blog for a short time until I realized that I just didn't have enough time to dedicate to it, with all the other family, ministry and writing projects I was involved in. However when the 2012-13 season ended, I was a bit burned out. Life was happening, our ninth child was on the way, my family and I were planning a cross country relocation and I simply disappeared from the forums and websites I had once so passionately haunted.

Life is still happening and now just eight months after relocating and getting all settled in we are once again in an entirely different locale (after yet another long and strenuous relocation), this time settling into a recently purchased home we would like to actually live in for more than 12 months.

However, although life is still as unpredictable as ever, the 2013-14 NBA season is almost finished, the Boston Celtics are an enigma after trading franchise savior's Paul Pierce and Kevin Garnett and signing a coach who looks like he could be playing ball on my 14 year old son's team in Brad Stevens (a great hire in my mind by the way), and, most importantly, the Celtics have the pieces necessary (expiring contracts, cap space, draft picks and talented tradeable players) to build an NBA championship level roster in short order. At a time like this, how could I not write about the Celtics?

As for where the idea for a *Be the General Manager* and *Choose your Own Ending Sports Adventure* book came from, such is an easy question to answer. My children and even I myself have always enjoyed *Choose Your Own Adventure* books and I have been the quintessential arm-chair General Manager for years now; simply put, I was bound to write a book like this someday. And, with the Celtics having the necessary pieces to recreate their entire team and turn one of the worst teams in 2013-14 into one of the best teams in 2014-15 I thought now was the perfect time to write this book. Of course, it also made perfect sense to write this book after having recently finished *Saving the Lakers: A Be the General Manager Book*, so there's that too.

Anyways, my hope is that young and old Celtics fans, stat-geeks, number-crunchers, arm-chair GM's and just plain basketball fans alike will enjoy this book and read it again and again and again, until they make all the correct choices necessary to win the championship. The truth is that winning the title on one's first read-through of this book is much, much, much harder to do than winning the NBA title is for any player in the league today, period.

There are only 30 teams in the league which means that every team starts the season with a 1-in-30 chance of winning the title or 30/1 odds. However, in order to win the championship in this book, you will have to beat incredible odds. How incredible you ask? Simply put, you literally have a better chance of actually playing in the NBA than you have of winning the title on your first read-through of this book; yes, I'm serious!

The odds that you win the title on your first read through of this book are exactly 995,330 / 1. That's right nine- hundred and ninty-five thousand, three-hundred and thirty to one! You literally have a .00000100469 percent chance of winning the title on your first read through of this book!

Simply put, there are about 80 countries on the face of planet earth whose entire populations could read and try to win the title on their first read through of this book without even one single citizen doing so. In the good ole U.S.A, if every single one of its 317,000,000 citizens, including the comatose, infants and Otis Smith, read this book, a whopping 318 people would be able to win the title on their first read-through. In comparison there are well over 500 players and coaches in the NBA today. Think about that. No seriously, really think about that; it's insane!

If you can conquer this book and win the title on your first, or even your tenth read-through, you could be a real life NBA General Manager one day. I honestly believe that, especially considering Otis Smith was once hired as a General Manager. All of that said, read carefully, chose wisely, stay true to who you are, make the decisions you feel will help the team win the 2014-15 NBA title ... and don't forget to have fun!

PROLOGUE

I remember the first time I ever met a black person in-person, or perhaps I should say, I remember the first time I ever met a black person I remember meeting in-person. Her name was Tara Weston and she took my breath away.

I had just moved to the city with my mom after she left my country bumpkin dad (I say this in love as I adore that country bumpkin) to play the field and take a higher paying job when I was 8 years old. I had seen a few black people on television growing up, namely the *Huxtables* and the *Jeffersons* as well as some athletes. However, since we only owned a television for perhaps a total of ten months out of my first eleven years of life, I can't really remember seeing any other black people, even on television, other than athletes. Dominique Wilkins was my favorite athlete, followed by Charles Barkley, Isaih Thomas and Dennis Rodman.

From just about the first moment I laid eyes on Tara, I must have unconsciously determined that black women were more attractive than white women, period. I say this because from the time I met Tara until the moment I meant my wife to be, upwards of ninety percent of the women I had crushes on or found extremely attractive were black. My wife (who is Caucasian and of French/English/German descent) often jokes, *I'm so happy you married me even though I was white.* There are no secrets between us and I often think she knows me better than I know myself.

To this day, if I had to create an NBA style 15 member team of the most *physically* attractive women of all time, my wife would be one of only four white women on the team, along with Raquel Welch, Monica Bellucci (whom my wife resembles) and Elle MacPherson. The remaining 11 members would be (in no particular order): Serena Williams, Vivica A. Fox, Beyonce Knowles, Paige Thomas (from season 2 of *X-Factor* USA), Kym Whitley, Nia Long, Cindy Herron, Onika Maraj (aka Nicki Minaj), Rosario Dawson, Paula Patton and Kim Kardashian. The team would be coached by Monica Potter, as if she can almost become Mayor of Berkeley (even if it was while playing *Kristina Braverman* on the best show on television, *Parenthood*) she could lead a team full of divas. Besides, I nearly fall in love with her every time I watch an old episode of *Boston Legal*.

However, I would make sure I also had Pam Grier, Adina Howard, Whitney Houston, Dana Owens (aka Queen Latifah), Tasha Smith, Deidra Roper (aka Spindarella), Jessica Alba, Jennifer Lopez, Vanessa Bryant (Kobe Bryant's wife), Brenda Song and Freida Pinto, as well as Caucasians Charlize Theron, Liv Tyler, Gemma Arterton and Cindy Crawford on my 15 member D-League affiliate. This team would be coached by Bridget Moynahan, as if she can handle herself in the New York District Attorney's Office (even if such only happens when she is acting as *Erin Reagan* in *Blue Bloods*) she could also lead a team full of divas. Besides, I also nearly fall in love with her every time I watch an episode of *Blue Bloods* as well, and personally I think Tom Brady was insane for choosing Gisele Bundchen over her!

Needless to say, I have no doubt my NBA and D-league teams would sell more tickets than any other teams in their respective sports. And, for the record, my star cheerleader would be Janet Jackson (I still remember watching the *Love will Never Do Without You* video on *BET* when I was 11 years old and just being blown away). And, the only announcer I would ever hire would be Jenifer Lewis, as in my mind, she has the greatest *voice* of all time, and it doesn't hurt that she is gorgeous as well.

For those keeping track at home, out of the 30 women on my two NBA style teams, 15 were black, eight were white, four were Latina, one was Armenian, one was Indian, one was Asian, and a great many would be considered of *mixed* ancestry. It would be next to impossible for me to *rank* these 30 women in any concrete way as the order would undoubtedly change constantly. However, I will say that my concrete *Fabulous Four*, in order, is:

1. My wife – seriously.
2. Serena Williams
3. Kym Whitley
4. Vivica A. Fox

I can also say that Monica Bellucci, Beyonce Knowles, Kim Kardashian and Paula Patton would be a lock for my Top 10 list no matter what day it was. Elle MacPherson, Rosario Dawson, Paige Thomas and Onika Maraj (aka Nicki Minaj) would fight it out for the tenth spot on most days.

Anyone reading this should be able to see the above lists are anything but sexist and that they are merely my honest opinion. Every woman on the planet is *attractive* in one way or another, and outside of the majority of my 15 member first team being black, there really is no defining physical characteristic each of the members on either team have. Just try to compare Kym Whitley with Cindy Herron or Rosario Dawson with Serena Williams or Monica Bellucci with Nia Long on the first team, or Dana Owens (aka Queen Latifah) with Freida Pinto or Tasha Smith with Brenda Song on the second team; such would be an exercise in futility to say the least!

In fact, compare my Top 30 list with the top 30 women listed on *FHM's 2014 Official 100 Sexiest Women in the World* where 27 of the top 30 are Caucasian and just two are black; two, now that is ridiculous!

I realize that Vivica A. Fox may no longer be the traffic stopping beauty she was in her 20s and that she's almost 50 years old now. But, she didn't even make the Top 100 while Caucasian Nigela Lawson, who *FHM* ranked #21 is 54 years old already! Something is just not right about that.

All of the above said and in all seriousness (I don't expect Vivica A. Fox to make it onto a list of the *Sexiest* women in the year 2014 at nearly 50 years old), the fact is that physical beauty is indeed found in all races, colors, shapes and sizes, and that beauty is indeed *in the eye of the beholder*! However, beauty is also *fleeting* and the most important characteristic any woman can truly have is that of a pure and beautiful spirit. That said, God's *Top 30* list could indeed be filled with woman that most men on this planet would not find *physically* attractive in any way, shape or form, and yet they would be the most beautiful of all!

Being a white kid originally from a small rural town, with only white relatives, some of whom were racist (though not my mom or dad) and enrolled in a High School that had a large contingent of self-proclaimed *hicks from the sticks*, the fact that I was primarily attracted to black classmates, had black friends, played hoops for probably a solid 25-35 hours per week, wore *Cross Colors* clothing, pimp walked and listened to 2PAC religiously, you can imagine I heard my fair share of *ni*g*r lover* and *wigger* (i.e. white ni*g*r) insults. However, such ignorant words never bothered me as I knew the people who spoke them were merely filled with hatred and in need of education and enlightenment.

I suppose my mom and dad deserve some credit as well, though I wouldn't have thought so at the time. My mom had left my dad and ended up dating multiple black men and almost marrying one of them (until he cheated on her – you reap what you sow). She even dated a man who had dated one of my classmates which grossed me out to no end. However, while I didn't approve of her leaving my dad, let alone of acting like a teenager and needing me to be the parent in the house, I most definitely did learn tolerance from her. As for my dad, he was a bumpkin, loved rock 'n' roll music, wore plaid shirts and tight jeans and loved Chuck Norris movies. However, he was also an extremely loving, caring and tolerant man who stood by his principles no matter what anyone else thought and was the type of man that would give a stranger the shirt of his back if necessary. When he was in High School back in the early '70s he took a black girl on a date and went for a stroll with her down by the boardwalk. A group of men saw him, jumped him and beat him so bad that he was hospitalized with broken ribs, though as my dad is quick to mention, not before he knocked a couple of them out and threw another one over the railing into the river below. Needless to say, I am my parents' child.

Even before I repented of my sins, believed on the Lord and Savior Jesus Christ of Nazareth and dedicated my life to my Creator, thereby understanding there was an actual divine reason to detest racism and an unchangeable code to live by that forbid racism of any kind, I simply couldn't wrap my mind around how anyone with a brain could hate, or even mildly dislike, someone else simply because of the color of his or her skin. Even though I was originally a *boy from the sticks*, such racist idiocy made no sense to me.

I did have racist relatives however, some of whom did not consider themselves racist, which basically sums up Donald Sterling in the minds of many. Now and then I would hear one of them tell a joke or make a racist remark and I would quickly jump down their throat and express my disgust with such. That didn't seem to stop them but at least they knew I disapproved.

However, perhaps I should have physically attacked the individuals who spoke such *words*, or cursed them and everyone associated with them (as Calvin Broadus, aka Snoop Dogg, aka Snoop Lion recently did to Donald Sterling), or keyed their car, or stole money out of their purse or wallet when they weren't looking? No, I don't think any of that would have been called for. Two wrongs don't make a right and rewarding evil with evil is never wise, period.

When someone uttered *words* that offended me I uttered *words* that let them know I was disgusted with their behavior. That seemed like an appropriate response to me then. I still feel the same way today.

That's just the way it is ... I see no changes. All I see is rac-ist faces. Misplaced hate makes disgrace to races, we un-der, I wonder what it takes to make this one better place? Let's erase the wasted. Take the evil out the people, they'll be acting right ... And only time we chill is when we kill each other; it takes skill to be real, time to heal each other ... Some things will never change.
- Changes, Tupac Amaru Shakur aka *2PAC*

In *Changes*, Pac does not condemn racism as much as he admits it exists and challenges his listeners to re-move the *evil* from themselves, act right and *heal* others. When the world heard Donald Sterling's voice on the in-famous recordings released by TMZ and Deadspin, did they remove *evil* from their own heart, *act right* and try to *heal* Mr. Sterling and others? Or, did they reward evil with evil, act with their emotions rather than with reason and logic, and do anything but help try to heal Mr. Ster-ling or anyone else?

People can say whatever negative things they want about Tupac Shakur; I love him, respect him, consider him an artistic genius and happily credit him with con-tributing to my own dogged quest to remain true to myself no matter what anyone else thinks. Pac was a ghetto prophet as well as an enlightened soul; I truly believe that. He was also a tortured soul and someone who, like the Biblical Paul of Tarsus, could say, *for what I would, that do I not; but what I hate, that do I (Romans 7: 15b)*. I can say the same. In fact, I think we all can, if we are honest with ourselves, whether our name is Donald Ster-ling, Barack Obama or any other name under the sun.

Martin Luther King, Jr. once wrote, while in jail for committing nonviolent civil disobedience during the Montgomery bus boycott:

We must develop and maintain the capacity to forgive. He who is devoid of the power to forgive is devoid of the power to love. There is some good in the worst of us and some evil in the best of us. When we discover this, we are less prone to hate our enemies. Forgiveness does not mean ignoring what has been done or putting a false label on an evil act. It means, rather, that the evil act no longer remains as a barrier to the relationship. Forgiveness is a catalyst creating the atmosphere necessary for a fresh start and a new beginning.
- From The Class of Nonviolence, prepared by Colman McCarthy of the Center for Teaching Peace, 4501 Van Ness Street, NW, Washington, D.C. 20016 202/537-1372).

Martin Luther King, Jr. was also a modern prophet, yet far too often his words are ignored by the very people he was trying to lead out of bondage (blacks with their bondage to oppression and unforgiveness and whites with their bondage to oppressing others and lack of true love for their fellow man), just as Moses words were ignored by the Israelites he lead out of Egypt, or Jesus' words were ignored by nearly everyone who heard Him. God sends the prophets to the earth and they are almost always rejected. This is to our shame.

MLK, like Tupac before him and Paul of Tarsus before him, knew that there is indeed *good in the worst of us and evil in the best of us*. I have no doubt that MLK would have advised his listeners to reprimand Donald Sterling for his offensive *words* with loving *words* of wisdom and rebuke, not with the maniacal insults, threats and hatred that Mr. Sterling ended up receiving.

There is *good* in Donald Sterling, of this I have no doubt. He has done a great deal more for a great many people than many of us would do for the same, and that isn't even debatable. Of course, there is also *evil* in Donald Sterling, and of this I also have no doubt. He has committed adultery which is a damnable sin for one (of course the NBA could care the less if one is committing a damnable sin, as such a sin is commonplace in the immoral age we find ourselves in and the NBA is concerned with money more so than morality). He is human, period. We all are.

MLK taught that when we realize there is *good in the worst of us and evil in the best of us* we are less prone to hate our enemies. I agree with him and can only assume that those individuals who lashed out at Donald Sterling did so because they are consumed with self-righteousness and feel there is no *evil* in their own heart. That or they are simply being hypocritical. Either way, such actions are to their shame.

MLK also taught that once one truly forgives, there will be no barrier to forming a relationship with the offending party and that a new beginning is possible for both parties. That is exactly what Tupac was teaching when he said, *Take the evil out the people, they'll be acting right ... it takes skill to be real, time to heal each other.* Tupac was teaching people to look in the mirror and remove the *evil* from their own hearts, so that they could then start to *heal* others rather than merely compounding the problem and escalating the situation.

Martin Luther King and Tupac Shakur taught the same thing; crazy but true. The question is, will you listen to them, or is your hatred for Donald Sterling's supposed views and beliefs and therefore Donald Sterling himself, so great that you cannot forgive, cannot remove the *evil* from yourself, cannot *act right* and cannot *heal*?

If the latter is the case, please consider the words of Jesus Christ of Nazareth, the One who loved you enough to live a sinless yet thankless life on this earth, be tortured and ultimately crucified, and finally rise again to prove He had conquered death and hell, leaving you a perfect example to emulate and aspire too. For it was Jesus who said:

For if ye forgive men their trespasses,
your heavenly Father will also forgive you:
But if ye forgive not men their trespasses,
neither will your Father forgive your trespasses.

ABOUT THE AUTHOR

Bryant T. Jordan, or BTJ as many known him, is a free-lance writer, author & creator of the innovative *Be the General Manager Book* series published by Sports Seer Publishing LLC.

BTJ does not write from the perspective of a *team fan* but from that of a sports realist and logician. His is a voice of clarity in a field filled with rabid-team fans and even professional writer's manic emotionalism.

BTJ lives in a rural paradise with his high-school sweetheart and wife of 17 plus years, as well as his magnificent children, under the amazing care of His God and Savior. He considers himself the most blessed man on the planet, period.

www.Bryant T Jordan.com

www.ingramcontent.com/pod-product-compliance
Lightning Source LLC
Chambersburg PA
CBHW070547030426
42337CB00016B/2395